ISBN:979-8-9906692-0-8 | **Library of Congress No.** 2024910202

E-book: ISBN 979-8-9906692-1-5

Scripture quotations marked **KJV** from the King James Version of the Bible.

Scripture quotations marked **NKJV** are from the New King James Version Copyright 1979, 1980, 1982 Thomas Nelson. All rights reserved.

Scripture quotations marked **ESV** English Standard Version® Copyright 2001 by Crossway.

Scripture's quotations marked **NIV** taken from the Holy Bible, New International Version®. Copyright © 1973, 1978, 1984 International Bible Society. Used by permission of Zondervan. All rights reserved.

To order additional copies, please visit:
https://www.garyraymin.com

When you order directly from Gary, he will sign it and ship it!

Painters Dream Productions is a Book Publisher dedicated to providing publishing services at affordable prices, helping to elevate our Author's work. **https://www.PaintersDream.com (931) 304-1359**

Painters Dream
PRODUCTIONS

Website Design | Audio Video Production | Social Media Marketing | Book Publishing

TABLE OF CONTENTS

RELIGION
Man's way of trying to
prove how good we are.

CHRISTIANITY
God's way of showing man
how loving He is.

FORWARDS by Bobby Howard & Bishop Steve Warren

Men of God must have a vision! King Solomon wrote, "Where there is no vision the people perish." Dr Gary Ray is a man of God with vision! As I perused this manuscript, I could sense his heart for the 21st Century Church. Traveling across the country lately, Dr. Ray has had a firsthand account of the condition of the church.

We hear the messages on television, read them in magazines, and realize that the church has strayed from the original meaning God gave her!! Dr. Ray gives specifics to this problem. He will open your eyes to the false doctrines that have filled the church. He will give you solutions to the problem.

When you see a car going the wrong way down the road you know problems are ahead. When we see the church on the "wrong side of Jesus" we know problems are ahead! Dr. Ray identifies these issues and calls them out to you, the reader.

Much sweat, tears, and prayer preceded this book. Words like this do not fall into the pages. The writer must know some will be offended and some will shout Hallelujah!! God is speaking through His anointed servant to rally the church to repentance and speak the truth. May your heart be challenged. May your vision return. May the Church of God be blessed by the efforts of this dear man of God as he shares his heart!

Bobby Howard
Pastor of "The Father's House" Lavergne, TN.
Founding Member of the "Jerry Goff Trio."

But this is a people robbed and plundered; All of them are snared in holes, and they are hidden in prison houses; They are for prey, and no one delivers; for plunder, and no one says, "RESTORE!" **(ISAIAH 42:22) NKJV**

"Throughout the Bible, God has raised up prophets for direction, guidance, inspiration, and correction. Just like in the book of Exodus chapter 9, when God spoke to Moses to go to Pharaoh and command to let His people go.

Also, in I Kings chapter 17 as God sent Elijah to the woman of Zarephath, when the widow woman and her son needed a miracle just to eat. God raised up John, in Luke chapter 14 as God sent him to the highways and hedges to compel them to come in.

Dr. Gary Ray is a man sent from God with a word directly from the throne for this last age. This book will definitely be an eye opener to the church.

I believe God has touched the heart of this prophet to align us for the second coming of the Lord Jesus Christ.

As you read this book, I believe that it is more than just a shelf collector, but will be truths that will set you free, and I highly recommend it for the church of today."

Bishop Steve Warren
Pastor of Faith Chapel Ministries,
Baxter, TN.

INTRODUCTION

As I endeavored to put this book together, my goal was to let us look behind the veil. Even though the curtain was rent from top to bottom, there are things that we should see and realize their importance. Some who read it will receive it and some won't.

I knew some time ago this book needed to be written, but it had to be in God's timing, and not mine. I am convinced that the time has come, I hope this book will encourage and inspire those who read it. **NOW is the time for some things to be revealed concerning the church (and they are not pretty).**

Apostasy and compromise have become the agenda of the Church today! As we go further, we will see a firm picture of the condition of the church.

> *Now the Spirit expressly says that **in latter times** <u>some</u> will depart from the faith, giving heed to deceiving spirits and doctrines of demons, speaking lies in hypocrisy, having their own conscience seared with a hot iron, forbidding to marry, and commanding to abstain from foods which God created to be received with thanksgiving by those who believe and know the truth.* **(1 Timothy 4:1-3) NKJV**

The Bride of Christ is not pure like our Lord commanded! We compromised and sold our birthright for a bowl of slop!

> *But know this, that in the last days perilous times will come: For men will be lovers of themselves, lovers of money, boasters, proud, blasphemers, disobedient to parents, unthankful, unholy, unloving, unforgiving, slanderers, without self-control, brutal, despisers of good, traitors, headstrong, haughty, lovers of pleasure rather than lovers of God, having a form of godliness but denying its power. And from such people turn away!* **(2 Timothy 3:1-5) NKJV**

It should shock us to see what the condition of the church is now. I was thinking back to when I was growing up in the church, and today coming to terms with the fact that I am a seventh-generation preacher. My dad, my uncle, my granddad, great granddad, and two more grandparents behind them. I have seen how the church operates, and it is nothing new to me.

I watched my dad struggle to pastor those small churches, working a full-time job out of town and being gone from home from Monday morning until Friday night. I believe there are better ways to serve the congregation.

After 40 years in full-time ministry, I have a concept of what God intended for the church to be and look like. It's sad to say this is not what I see now. I watched my dad, and so many of the other preachers that I was raised with struggle to compete with deacons in the church who thought their job was to pick the pastors, and then tell them how they should run the church. **WRONG!**

In studying the Bible somehow or another, deacons took on a responsibility that was never theirs in the first place. Worse, they never consulted the Word of God to see what their responsibilities as deacons were to be. In the Bible, a deacon's responsibilities were to take care of the finances and the needs of the widows and orphans of the church. See for yourself!

> *Now in those days, when the disciples was multiplying, there arose a complaint against the Hebrews by the Hellenists,* ***because their widows were neglected*** *in the daily distribution. Then the twelve summoned the multitude of the disciples and said, "It is not desirable that we should leave the word of God and serve tables." Therefore, brethren, seek out from among you seven men of reputation, full of the Holy Spirit and wisdom, whom we may appoint over this business; But we will give ourselves continually to prayer and to the ministry of the word."* **(ACTS 6:1-4) NKJV**

If Christians in the church would:
- Humble Themselves
- Pray
- Seek God's face
- Turn from their wicked ways

I'm convinced that God would send the Pastor/Teacher that the church desperately needs. I have seen many times that when Christians would seek God's face in any situation, He always answered.

One good example of what prayer will do is this.

I remember the Brownsville revival that took place at the Brownsville Assembly of God in Pensacola, Florida. I remember talking and hearing from different people how they went to this revival hoping to bring it back to their church, but it never happened. The reason it didn't happen is that God is an originator. He never reproduces himself.

If you were to do a bit of checking into this revival, you would find that somebody was praying in the church 24 hours a day, seven days a week for 2 1/2 years <u>before</u> this revival happened.

**If there is to be another move of God,
even greater than that one,
I believe it could happen:**

But it only will when men and women who have had an experience with God and have given their life to him, consecrate themselves, to pray and to seek His face.

Most people who attend church today are too involved in their jobs, their interests, and anything else that comes down the pike. We must sacrifice whatever it takes to dedicate the time and effort to get close enough to God to accomplish His will.

It won't happen again until people in the churches are willing to consecrate themselves and spend time in prayer for this to happen again. This is the answer to when this will take place.

Let us look at the Bible for our answer.

> *If My people who are called by My name will humble themselves, and pray and seek My face, and turn from their wicked ways,* **then I will hear from heaven and will forgive their sin and heal their land.**
> **(2 Chronicles 7:14) NKJV**

The above Scripture just gave us the answer. If you're looking for a real move of God, this is what it will take, **PERIOD.** You can see there are a lot of different situations concerning the church that we will deal with in this book. This is just one of those things. As I said before, not all of them are going to be pretty.

If we as the church have any desire for the deliverance of the church, real revival, and healing to come to our land, then we should not be ashamed to deal with them in Truth. For so many years we have been willing to just accept things as they were, knowing even in the end that the Bible said something different than what was being preached and taught in the church. The main reason pastors have transitioned into this way of doing things is to see the numbers of the congregation go up, therefore making the tithes increase. Did the LORD not say?

> *I will build my* **church,** *and the gates of Hades will not overcome it.* (**MATTHEW 16:18**) **KJV**

For so long many leaders in the churches have been regurgitating what they have learned from TV preachers. They tell us how to live our lives, how to move in the spirit, and all the other things that churches traditionally do. They don't realize they don't have any true God-given knowledge. They only know what they learned and heard from men before them, and not directly from the Word of God.

My people are destroyed for lack of knowledge. Because you have rejected knowledge, I also will reject you from being priest for Me; Because you have forgotten the law of your God, I also will forget your children. **(Hosea 4:6) NKJV**

I believe in many cases, the spirit the church is operating in now is a religious/legalistic spirit, not the Holy Spirit. That is why we aren't seeing people saved, healed, or dedicated to the work of the Lord. One major hindrance in the church today is "that's the way Daddy and Mama always did it, so that's the way it is supposed to be done." We don't want to ever forget the things that we were taught growing up, but as we become adults and then Christian adults.

We should pray for God to speak to us
and give us an understanding of His Word.

If you have not already figured it out, I was raised hard shell, foot-washing, once saved always saved. I had trouble with this for a long time because it was a deceptive way that the enemy had to be able to deceive people into believing they could do anything and get by. We definitely will go deeper into this as we progress in the book, so get ready. After I became filled with the Holy Spirit with the evidence of speaking in tongues, and became affiliated with the Pentecostal denomination, I began to realize that some things are just not the way I had been made to believe they were.

CHAPTER 1
GODS INTENTIONS FOR HIS CHURCH

In this chapter, we will deal with God's intended purpose for his church.

First, what is the church according to the Old Testament?

The word translated "church" in the English Bible is ekklesia. This word is the Greek word kaleo (to call), with the prefix ek (out). Thus, the word means **"the called-out ones."** However, the English word "church" does not come from ekklesia but from the word kuriakon, which means "dedicated to the Lord."

There seems to be a lot of confusion in most cultures, including my own when it comes to church today. If you were to listen to people speaking about the church, it becomes obvious that most peoples' understanding concerning the church is usually connected to a building and is always tied to all the things that happen in that building.

Now we paint the walls black and the ceiling too and make it dark inside. First of all, God is not the God of darkness. He is the God of light. The church has just become simply smoke and mirrors to impress the people with what we can produce in the flesh, not what we can produce in the Spirit, the Spirit of God.

There is nothing that could be further from the biblical image of what God intended for His church to look like. Could I just clear up one thing before we go any further? That is, the building that we put so much faith and hope in is not the church.

If this were the case for the early followers of Jesus when He was walking on this earth, they would have been in trouble, because there were no church buildings.

When Jesus made the statement *"It is important that I go away,"* He realized that if He stayed here, He could only reach those to whom He could minister.

So, to fulfill God's plan for man, He sent a comforter, the Holy Spirit to live (dwell) in us. The church is internal. It is in you, the Christian and the kingdom that God speaks about us building is external.

Let us look at Jesus, or, if you go back and do just a little bit of studying, you'll find out that Jesus is called the *"second Adam."* Why did God call him the *"second Adam?"*

**It was so that through Him
we could receive back
what had been lost
in the garden by the first Adam.**

We must first realize it was not to be called a church. It was to be called a (HOUSE OF PRAYER). This building that we call a church should be filled with people who pray together, eat together, and live their lives together.

If there was any ministry that needed help at that time, they would take what they had, either to give to the needy or sell what they had and if necessary, give to the needy.

They were willing to sacrifice their lives for one another. These ways are foreign and strange to people in the church today. The people in our churches today are too busy with work and recreation. Worst of all, too many church people are mad or at odds with other church people to spend time with each other.

**We will not find the word
church in the Old Testament.
God's chosen people, Israel,
was His church on that day.**

Here is where you begin to see where the Lord speaks to Abram He says:

> go from your country, your people and your father's household to the land I will show you. I will make you into a great nation, and I will bless you; I will make your name great, and you will be a blessing. I will bless those who bless you, and whoever curses you I will curse; and all the peoples on earth will be blessed through you. **(Genesis 12:1-3) KJV**

Here is where we first see God's intention to gather Himself to a particular people who would become His representation in this world. The phrase *"So that you will be a blessing,"* is not just a statement about what will be. It is a statement about what **must be**.

When God began to demonstrate His true nature and character, His message became alive with His vision of the church. His intended purpose was to accomplish this through a community of people. The greater context of Scripture confirms this through the prophet Isaiah when he says.

> I am the LORD; **I have called you** in righteousness; **I will** take you by the hand and keep you; **I will** give you as a covenant(why?)for the people, a light for the nations, to open the eyes that are blind, to bring out the prisoners from the dungeon, from the prison those who sit in darkness. **(Isaiah 42:6-7) ESV**

Now let us move on to God's intended purpose for the church in the New Testament. We will find the beginning of the Church in the New Testament.

> You are the salt of the earth. But if the salt loses its saltiness, how can it be made salty again? It is no longer good for anything, except to be thrown out and trampled underfoot. "You are the light of the world. A town built on a hill cannot be hidden. **(Matthew 5:13-14) NIV**

This speaks of the disciples' major influence and impact on the world. And the word "church" is yet to be used in the bible. Seeing God's people begin to take part in His direction and movement of His people is as clear as it could be.

The true purpose of the church from Abram to Jesus, His people are always shown as moving outward to be able to help others as they witness Christ, and His Kingdom, and His presence. With every page you turn His movement will come into view, and we will begin to see the church being born. We will start to see the reason for the creation of the church.

I don't want to talk about this again until we get to the end of the book, but just to give you a quick look there was a little chapel in New York City that was the only building that was not destroyed on September 11, 2001. If we were to go back in history, we would find this little chapel that was the place where our first president, George Washington worshiped. Let us understand the importance of this little chapel during the period before the Twin Towers fell.

In the book of Isaiah, Chapter 9, that was a time when the Assyrians defeated the children of Israel.

They decided to rebuild, but not using the plan God had for them. They altered the way they wanted to build. Does that not sound like the church today? Even though it had been built with sycamore trees, it seemed right that since they had all been depleted, they determined to rebuild it with a stone, hewn out.

They also decided to use cedar trees, which was definitely against God's plan, consequently, it didn't work. How many times, since you have been a Christian, has God spoken to you to do something in your church, or outside the church, and you, after thinking about it, decided you had a better way to do it?

We get in trouble so many times
by trying to do things our way.

CHAPTER 2

THE BEGINNING OF THE NT CHURCH

The former account I made, O Theophilus, of all that Jesus began both to do and teach, until the day in which He was taken up, after He through the Holy Spirit had given commandments to the apostles whom He had chosen, to whom He also presented Himself alive after His suffering by many infallible proofs, being seen by them during forty days and speaking of the things pertaining to the kingdom of God. And being assembled together with them, He commanded them not to depart from Jerusalem, but to wait for the Promise of the Father, "which," He said, "you have heard from Me; for John truly baptized with water, but you shall be baptized with the Holy Spirit not many days from now." Therefore, when they had come together, they asked Him, saying, "Lord, will You at this time restore the kingdom to Israel?" And He said to them, "It is not for you to know times or seasons which the Father has put in His own authority. But you shall receive power when the Holy Spirit has come upon you; and you shall be witnesses to Me in Jerusalem, and in all Judea and Samaria, and to the end of the earth." **(ACTS 1:1-8) NKJV**

Now it's in Acts chapter 1, verse 12 where this promised meeting takes place. They then returned to Jerusalem and went into the place where they were staying. They went up into the upper room.

There was Peter, James, John, and Andrew, Philip and Thomas, Bartholomew and Matthew, James the son of Alphaeus and Simon the son of James. All of these men continued with one accord in prayer and supplication. Also, there were women, and Mary the mother of Jesus, and with his brothers in all there were 120 in that room, and they stayed there until the promise came.

This was a miraculous thing that took place. They were all in one accord in one place, and suddenly there came a sound from heaven as if of a rushing mighty wind. It then filled the whole place where they were.

Then there appeared tongues of fire that rested on each of them, and they were filled with the Holy Spirit and began to speak in other languages as the Spirit gave them utterance. When they left that place, I believe that's where the church in the New Testament was born.

When they left and went out, the Word says that they went from house to house. This is where it became a house of prayer. They also were willing to sell all that they had to be able to supplement those in need, and what they had to have. There wasn't any selfishness, or any big I's and little you's. Everything and everyone were equal.

> There is neither Jew nor Greek, there is neither slave nor free, there is neither male nor female; **for you are all one in Christ Jesus.** **(Galatians 3:28) NKJV**

CHAPTER 3

THE BEGINNING OF THE END

Here is where things began to change in the church. I know that it started way before this, but I want to start in the 1960s.

First, Benjamin Spock wrote his baby book that began to instruct us on how to raise our children. He taught against hard discipline so that we as parents don't kill their spirits.

A lot of "Christians" believed him, even though this was strictly against the Word of God.

Look at our children and young people today. They are a messed-up group of people, living like the devil, and believing that there will be no repercussions for what they do. Parents and teachers, their lives will rest on our heads in judgment.

I am certainly not saying that some children are taught right, and still go astray, most definitely. At the same time, we see the love generation again, with the attitude that if it feels good, do it.

Now, as the church begins to take its new place in the world, it's at this time that it begins to look for a way to justify what each denomination would believe. Here we see the charismatic or the way I describe it "Charis-maniac" movement that brings a more radical religious concept, with its radical beliefs as far as healing, demonic deliverance, and things of this nature.

I hope you will understand, here is where I feel like the church began to get off track. There's more to say than what we have been taught, and as we go on, I will try to share some of that with you.

It was at this point, in the setting up of the charismatic movement, that certain men gained control and began to establish the way things were to operate.

This is when the faith movement, as it operates now, began, and brought in the prosperity message and the modernization of the church.

We now know that this is not true, and many ministers are denouncing their participation in that, and I feel that there will be many more to come.

In view of all this, make every effort to respond to God's promises. Supplement your faith with a generous provision of moral excellence, and moral excellence with knowledge, and knowledge with self-control, and self-control with patient endurance, and patient endurance with godliness, and godliness with brotherly affection, and brotherly affection with love for everyone. The more you grow like this, the more productive and useful you will be in your knowledge of our Lord Jesus Christ. But those who fail to develop in this way are shortsighted or blind, forgetting that they have been cleansed from their old sins. So, dear brothers and sisters, work hard to prove that you really are among those God has called and chosen. Do these things, and you will never fall away. Then God will give you a grand entrance into the eternal Kingdom of our Lord and Savior Jesus Christ. **(2 Peter 1:5-11) NLT**

I do believe that the Scripture that I've just added here is an answer to what faith is.

Faith shows the reality of what we hope for; it is the evidence of things we cannot see. Through their faith, the people in days of old earned a good reputation. By faith we understand that the entire universe was formed at God's command, that what we now see did not come from anything that can be seen. **(Hebrews 11:1-3) NLT**

I am always amazed at God's wisdom in how He made everything work so perfectly. Yet anytime man gets control of something that God has made he always messes it up. I don't know why but that is true.

We will begin to see the demise of the church. I did not realize how far the church had fallen until I began to look and listen to what God was telling me, and IT AIN'T PRETTY.

It is amazing what humans can do to mess up what God has made for good for the ones who simply love him. We have been able to mess that up also with all the different movements such as the Faith movement and the glory-ram.

CHAPTER 4

IS IT REAL OR IS IT MEMOREX?

Let's begin with the faith moment that has been so used, it's not that it's not real, it is. But the faith movement that we see has been abused so most people won't buy it anymore. They don't believe it's real. That's so sad because, unless I'm wrong, God still does the miraculous. He hasn't changed.

"For I am the Lord, I do not change." **(Malachi 3:6) NKJV**

Jesus Christ is the same yesterday, today, and forever. **(Hebrews 13:8) NKJV**

Preachers have a common means of gaining wealth such as houses and airplanes more than ministry. It became a status. The more you have, the bigger your ministry must be.

I can assure you that doesn't determine that God is within us, how big your ministry is, nor how much God will use you.

Remember your leaders who taught you the word of God. Think of all the good that has come from their lives and follow the example of their faith. Jesus Christ is the same yesterday, today, and forever. So do not be attracted by strange, new ideas. Your strength comes from God's grace, not from rules about food, which don't help those who follow them. **(HEBREWS 13:7-9) NLT**

The answer to this is that we have left our first love. Scripture has something to say about that.

But I have this complaint against you. You don't love me or each other as you did at first! **(REVELATION 2:4) NLT**

We spend so much of our time chasing after words and things that will make our life better and different and yet the only thing that's going to change it is us spending more time in His Word.

Hebrews 4:12 tells us:

For the word of God is alive and powerful. It is sharper than the sharpest two-edged sword, cutting between soul and spirit, between joint and marrow. It exposes our innermost thoughts and desires.

And…

God, who at various times and in various ways spoke in time past to the fathers by the prophets, has in these last days spoken to us by His Son… **(Hebrews 1:1-2) NKJV**

I just lost a good friend who battled cancer, but he never lost his faith. He trusted God even to the end and God revealed to me that this man lived out his faith.

Faith is believing in the Word, and it's somehow far above all the things we cannot see. It would be great if a man could give us that, but he can't. Only God can teach us the faith walk.

As for me, my life has already been poured out as an offering to God. The time of my death is near. I have fought the good fight, I have finished the race, and I have remained faithful. And now the prize awaits me—the crown of righteousness, which the Lord, the righteous Judge, will give me on the day of his return. And the prize is not just for me but for all who eagerly look forward to his appearing. **(2 TIMOTHY 4:7-8) NLT**

I'm convinced that if we would spend more time in His Word, studying, and applying it to our lives. We just might find our way back to where God wants His Church to be. Our brother Ezra said it best!

For Ezra had prepared his heart to seek[a] the Law of the Lord, and to do it, and to teach statutes and ordinances in Israel.
(Ezra 7:10) NKJV

Don't rush over this, it is the blueprint to a successful spiritual life.

Ezra prepared his heart to:

- Seek the law (The Bible at the time)
- Applied what he learned
- Taught it to others.

The church that we see today has painted the inside walls black and put all the fancy-colored lights, smoke machines, and lighting up the stage. All it is, is just smoke and mirrors.

When I go to one of these churches, God keeps saying He doesn't show up in the darkness. Please, He is a God of light. Did He not curse the darkness?

> *To open their eyes, so they may turn from darkness to light and from the power of Satan to God. Then they will receive forgiveness for their sins and be given a place among God's people, who are set apart by faith in me.* **(ACTS 26:18) NLT**

Somehow, I believe that leaders in the church think that they can out-thank God. Consequently, this is where the church has gone wrong. It's become the apostate church. The church that got in bed with the whore (the world).

> *Now I am no longer in the world, but these are in the world, and I come to You. Holy Father, keep through Your name those whom You have given Me, that they may be one as We are.* **(John 17:11) NKJV**

It pains me to say these things about the church that, as a boy, I was raised in. I can't say that they were right about everything that they did, but they were a lot closer than we are today.

I believe that those who are running the church have lost its vision, and its way.

There's no other way to see it. Let's look at the "glory movement." Please forgive me, but this is a real trip for me, people believe that gold dust is showing up in their hands and on them. Gems are showing up on the floor in the carpet, and feathers falling out of the air.

Let me ask a question, does this not bother you? I will tell you right now I have felt the anointing as strong as anybody, but I've never seen gold in my hands or any of the other things that the people in this movement say they witness. Have we ever stopped to think that the devil, our enemy, and adversary, cannot create these things to deceive the church?

I'm pretty sure by now that I'm in real trouble with the traditional and contemporary Christians, but people, what I'm looking for is a church without spots, wrinkles, or blemishes, which can create a change in the world that we're living in.

> *But the anointing which you have received from Him abides in you, and you do not need that anyone teach you; but as the same anointing teaches you concerning all things, and is true, and is not a lie, and just as it has taught you, you will abide in Him.* **(1 John 2:27) NKJV**

I have a pretty good sense of what the church should be or how it should be. I know they were old-fashioned in some sense and beautifully different in comparison to most of the newfangled churches, but I'm wondering if they weren't closer to what God intended the church to be.

Chapter 5

CHANGE DOES NOT COME EASY

I believe today that we are afraid to venture out and say this or that isn't right. It's time to make some necessary changes as to where the church is to go from here.

The Holy Spirit took me to the Holy of Holies the other night and showed me the things that a priest had to do at that time to simply go **behind the veil** into the presence of God.

He showed me how he had to cleanse and purify himself even before he put on the priestly garment that he was to wear to go behind the veil. He would then get his offering ready to put on the mercy seat, but before he was able to do that, he would burn incense that would be so thick that the Lord could not see his face, or the priest see the face of the Lord.

When they go into the tabernacle of meeting, or when they come near the altar to minister, to burn an offering made by fire to the Lord, they shall wash with water, lest they die. 21 So they shall wash their hands and their feet, lest they die. And it shall be a statute forever to them—to him and his descendants throughout their generations." **(Exodus 30:20-21) NKJV**

Look at what the NEW TESTAMENT SAYS:

If we confess our sins, He is faithful and just to forgive us our sins and to cleanse us from all unrighteousness. **(1 John 1:9) NKJV**

I am aware that when Jesus went to the Cross and made the statement "*it is finished*" the blood that he had shed for the sins of humanity and the veil at that point, was rent from top to bottom, which gave us access to the Holy of Holies.

And according to the law almost all things are purified with blood, and without shedding of blood there is no remission. **(Hebrews 9:22) NKJV**

We also see here things that the priest had to do in order just to present himself as acceptable to go behind the veil. They had to tie a rope around his ankle because if there was any sin found in him, he would die on the spot. So, we begin to see how important it is for a priest to have been acceptable.

The Bible says that the blood that Jesus shed on Calvary was enough for us to gain access to the presence of God, yet I am wondering if the way that men and women are called into ministry today is the way God intended it to be.

We have made it too easy to become a preacher. There are some things that we need to do that we haven't been doing, to be able to present ourselves worthy to stand behind those sacred desks and talk about God.

I think God is looking for some men who will present themselves holy and acceptable to the ministry of the gospel, and that it becomes important that we are reaching the lost at any cost.

It's not about building big works, and mega ministries. That's not what the ministry was ever to be about. It's about the lost and blind ones that are in need. I think it's time that we change our motives and begin to do the work that God has called us to do.

The last time that I preached God took me to Ezekiel chapter 7 verses 23 through 27. This is where the children of Israel were busy doing things their way, not God's way and to get them back in order He put them in captivity to the Babylonians.

I think this may be where the church is today. I made the statement the other day that I believe, because of the decisions the churches are making and the things that we are accepting and allowing into the church today, there's too much similarity in what was going on in Ezekiel's time to what's going on in the church today.

Take a look at the condition of the world. Pay attention to what's going on, and the fact that we have taken prayer out of school, and now we have digressed to the point that we are willing to allow our children to change their gender from boy to girl or girl to boy. What I see is the church doesn't even have the power to say how wrong that is.

We are now even allowing drag queens to come in and entertain our children and even have them join in. Come on Church, you can't find anywhere in the Word that justifies this.

We also are not afraid to commit murder anymore. The church can't stand up and even say killing your unborn baby is murder and is a sin.

Yes, I believe the woman's body belongs to her without question, but that still doesn't give her the right to take an innocent life. You can't make that right in anybody's book.

'*You shall not murder.* **(Deuteronomy 5:17) NKJV**

We need to take a stand IT'S NOT ABOUT FEELINGS, it's what the Bible says about marriage.

Therefore a man shall leave his father and his mother and hold fast to his wife, and they shall become one flesh. **(Genesis) 2:24 ESV**

All Scripture is given by inspiration of God, and is profitable for doctrine, for reproof, for correction, for instruction in righteousness, that the man of God may be complete, thoroughly equipped for every good work.
(2 Timothy 3:16-17) NKJV

These are not optional; it is clearly defined for our guidance. Sadly, the church wobbles back and forth trying to justify being able to marry two men or two women it just isn't right based on the Word.

Then there is the issue of homosexuality. We can't, as a body of believers, even determine how to deal with that issue. They say God is love, and He is. He loves everybody but He hates their lifestyle (sin).

The church's responsibility here is very simple. We don't throw anybody out of the church, but we don't allow anyone practicing this sin to take part in the church. Our responsibility is to get them delivered and saved.

I wrote a book titled "Deliverance the Final Release of The Church", and I believe that's where we are today. It's time we "submit to God, resist the devil and he will flee. He has to. He is still under command from God. God is Sovereign, NEVER FORGET THAT.

People say that because the church has lost its power it can't do that anymore. I say it's got to be brought back into the church.

The answer to all of this is found in Romans Chapter 1.

> *Paul, a servant of Jesus Christ, called to be an apostle, separated unto the gospel of God, (Which he had promised afore by his prophets in the holy scriptures,) Concerning his Son Jesus Christ our Lord, which was made of the seed of David according to the flesh; and declared to be the Son of God with power, according to the spirit of holiness, by the resurrection from the dead: by whom we have received grace and apostleship, for obedience to the faith among all nations, for his name: Among whom are ye also the called of Jesus Christ: To all that be in Rome, beloved of God, called to be saints: Grace to you and peace from God our Father, and the Lord Jesus Christ.*

> *First, I thank my God through Jesus Christ for you all, that your faith is spoken of throughout the whole world. For God is my witness, whom I serve with my spirit in the gospel of his Son, that without ceasing I make mention of you always in my prayers; making request, if by any means now at length I might have a prosperous journey by the will of God to come unto you.*

For I long to see you, that I may impart unto you some spiritual gift, to the end ye may be established; that is, that I may be comforted together with you by the mutual faith both of you and me. Now I would not have you ignorant, brethren, that oftentimes I purposed to come unto you, (but was let hitherto,) that I might have some fruit among you also, even as among other Gentiles.

I am debtor both to the Greeks, and to the Barbarians; both to the wise, and to the unwise. So, as much as in me is, I am ready to preach the gospel to you that are at Rome also. For I am not ashamed of the gospel of Christ: for it is the power of God unto salvation to every one that believeth; to the Jew first, and also to the Greek. For therein is the righteousness of God revealed from faith to faith: as it is written, The just shall live by faith. For the wrath of God is revealed from heaven against all ungodliness and unrighteousness of men, who hold the truth in unrighteousness; because that which may be known of God is manifest in them; for God hath shewed it unto them.

For the invisible things of him from the creation of the world are clearly seen, being understood by the things that are made, even his eternal power and Godhead; so that they are without excuse: because that, when they knew God, they glorified him not as God, neither were thankful; but became vain in their imaginations, and their foolish heart was darkened. Professing themselves to be wise, they became fools, and changed the glory of the uncorruptible God into an image made like to corruptible man, and to birds, and fourfooted beasts, and creeping things.

Wherefore God also gave them up to uncleanness through the lusts of their own hearts, to dishonour their own bodies between themselves: who changed the truth of God into a lie, and worshipped and served the creature more than the Creator, who is blessed for ever. Amen.

For this cause God gave them up unto vile affections: for even their women did change the natural use into that which is against nature: and likewise also the men, leaving the natural use of the woman, burned in their lust one toward another; men with men working that which is unseemly, and receiving in themselves that recompence of their error which was meet. And even as they did not like to retain God in their knowledge, God gave them over to a reprobate mind, to do those things which are not convenient; being filled with all unrighteousness, fornication, wickedness, covetousness, maliciousness; full of envy, murder, debate, deceit, malignity; whisperers, backbiters, haters of God, despiteful, proud, boasters, inventors of evil things, disobedient to parents, without understanding, covenant breakers, without natural affection, implacable, unmerciful who knowing the judgment of God, that they which commit such things are worthy of death, not only do the same, but have pleasure in them that do them.

It would be great if the church had taken a stand in the beginning based on the Word and stood for life. It would have been great, but as we look now, we realize the church doesn't have a vision and also no power either.

I realize as I write this book not everybody is going to be happy, but you know what, they will have to deal with that. I can't. I can only write what the Holy Spirit has directed me to write.

CHAPTER 6

THE CHURCH IN CONFINEMENT

I began to realize that like it was in the seventh chapter of Ezekiel when they were put in captivity under the Babylonian empire, maybe as I view the church that it is in captivity now that God said I've had enough, and I'll just let you have your way.

Something else that I've been wanting to say for so long in the church is we simply call people up front, have them repeat a prayer, and tell them that they are saved. I don't believe that will work any longer. Let me give you a piece of scripture to back that up.

> *No one can come to Me unless the Father who sent Me draws him; and I will raise him up at the last day.* **(JOHN 6:44) NKJV**

> *For by grace you have been saved through faith, and that not of yourselves; it is the gift of God, not of works, lest anyone should boast.* **(Ephesians 2:8-9) NKJV**

A great preacher, Bert Clendennen, made a statement. He said, "The fire will not fall on an empty altar."

I feel like we've made it too easy for people, but I wonder how many of those who walk forward really understand what it means to be saved. The scary part of that is that we, as preachers, will have their blood on our hands if we have watered down the truth or misled them. Just how many people sitting in the church pews are truly born again and have had a true experience? Too many preachers today share the bad news instead of the good news.

> *"Do not be afraid, for behold, I bring you good tidings of great joy which will be to all people."* **(Luke 2:10) NKJV**

Let's look at one more!

> *And how shall they preach unless they are sent? As it is written: "How beautiful are the feet of those who preach the gospel of peace, <u>Who bring glad tidings of good things!</u>"* **(Romans 10:15) NKJV**

There is something that has plagued me about this situation. I talked to a man of God the other day whom I trust, and I asked him this question. Those people who went to church searching for answers and went through the motions that the preacher told them to, really don't know if they had an experience or not. Where would they go if they die? If they're not truly saved, they'll go to hell. Is this not a scary thought?

> *For our gospel did not come to you in word only, but also in power, and in the Holy Spirit and in much assurance, as you know what kind of men we were among you for your sake.*
> **(1 Thessalonians 1:5) NKJV**

I think that we took out the most important piece of furniture in the church which is the altar, or the mercy seat. That means no one has a place to go to get victory over the burdens that they carry.

I will never forget, as a young boy 12 years old in a revival at Raysville Baptist Church in Moore County Tennessee, the church that my granddaddy built. I remember Brother Bryce Holder was preaching, and that conviction that we kept talking about drew me to that altar where I stayed until the burdens that I carried were lifted and I was set free.

I'm afraid many churches today are unaware of the spirit of conviction. I believe the reason is that what we see in the churches today is not the Holy Spirit with which we were raised. The "religious" seems to have inhabited the church, and now we realize that because of this we have lost our power and vision to accomplish the work of the real Gospel. There, I finally said it. It hurts me to realize that the church cannot change things as they are, but we are indeed in trouble and the church is unable to do anything about it.

Jesus said, *"Follow Me"*, not follow Christians.

• • •

I want to spend a few moments about something that is the scariest thing that I have ever seen, and that is the subversive tactics used today in the church by toxic ministries led by con men overseers.

Once I studied the subversive tactics the communist nations used to convert other nations into Socialism and then to Communism. I began to realize the tactics some so-called preachers had learned, they used to gain absolute control over their congregations.

We must realize that the result of these tactics is simply meant to bring about the one world government, which means the government is the overseer of the church. The church becomes just like the world. Do you hear this? We must realize what is happening to God's Church!

My wife, after reading what I had written so far, said to me "I think it's good but what are you going to say to make things better, or what will it take to rebuild the church and bring it back to the way God wanted it"? I believe she was right, so I'm going to close my book with this chapter on how we will restore the church to its former GLORY.

> *The Lord has spoken out against Jacob; his judgment has fallen upon Israel. And the people of Israel and Samaria, who spoke with such pride and arrogance, will soon know it. They said, "We will replace the broken bricks of our ruins with finished stone, and replant the felled sycamore-fig trees with cedars." But the Lord will bring Rezin's enemies against Israel and stir up all their foes.* **(ISAIAH:9:8-11) NLT**

Let me read a piece of Scripture that I think is important.

> *And I tell you that you are Peter, and on this rock I will build my church, and the gates of Hades will not overcome it.* **(MATTHEW 16:18) KJV**

Note what I underlined. He said, *"I will build my church."* He is doing the work IN AND THROUGH US! And church is singular. There is only 1 church and never forget He is building it using YOU!

As we move forward you will realize the importance of this Scripture. I'd like to look at September 9, 2011. This may be the most important story that I will tell you. I think this may be the very secret to rebuilding the church to its former glory.

I love in Isaiah Chapter 9 verse 10, the story of when the temple lay in ruins. They made the statement "We will rebuild it with hewn stones." The sycamores had been cut down, but we will change them to Cedars.

Let's look at September 11, 2001, again. You know there was an attack before 9/11 in the World Trade Center that did not bring the building down. They knew then that there would be another attack but did nothing about it.

When September 11, 2001, happened and the Twin Towers came down, the only building left standing was a little chapel, by the name of Saint Paul's Chapel, and the only thing that protected it from being destroyed was a sycamore tree. That sycamore tree is very important.

After they built the new building that they named the Freedom Tower, their plans in the beginning were to make it the tallest building in the world. Instead, they wound up making it the tallest building in the Western Hemisphere.

If we study their plan, we understand that they intended to make it bigger and better. Do you remember The Tower of Babel? They could have made it bigger and better, but God stopped it because men took control and took God out of it. Just like the men did on September 11, 2001, the men thought they could do it on their own. I believe the same thing has happened today. The church has left God out of it.

Again, it was a Sycamore tree that saved that chapel. After the Freedom Tower was built, they planted a cedar tree in front of it, and the cedar tree died.

I believe this is how we rebuild the church to its former glory. Righteousness exalts a nation. We can't substitute righteousness with unholy living.

I believe God wants quality not quantity.

We don't need any more programs. It's hard for me to admit my dad and those men who came before me had the solution to building the church. We should have listened. I believe the Word instructed us not to forsake the old paths. I think that's important.

> Thus says the Lord: *"Stand in the ways and see, And ask for the old paths, where the good way is, And walk in it; Then you will find rest for your souls. But they said, 'We will not walk in it.'* **(Jeremiah 6:16) NKJV**

We don't need any more smoke and mirrors or naked guitar players. What we need is the true and pure movement of the Holy Spirit; not a religious spirit that we see in the church today. I know it's hard, but we must change it now if we're going to make it.

> *For a long time Israel has been without the true God, without a teaching priest, and without law; but when in their trouble they turned to the Lord God of Israel, and sought Him, He was found by them. And in those times there was no peace to the one who went out, nor to the one who came in, but great turmoil was on all the inhabitants of the lands.* **(2 Chronicles 15:3-5) NKJV**

CHAPTER 7

LOOKING FROM BEHIND

I want to start this last chapter the same way I started the first chapter. "LET US TAKE A LOOK BEHIND THE VEIL".

If the church does not wake up, we're in trouble. It's the church that should have the power to save the world.

He said in the Scriptures.

"forsake not the old paths."

I believe the meaning here is that there are things that we can learn from our past mistakes that have been made, instead of just continually building off of these mistakes. If we continue this way nothing ever gets better.

I believe if we were to bring back the altar to the church where it belongs and begin to preach heaven is sweet and hell hot again and allow the true conviction to bring men and women to an old-fashioned altar, we would begin to see people saved and set free. The Spirit of God would change their lives forever.

> Then *if my people who are called by my name will humble themselves and pray and seek my face and turn from their wicked ways,* I will hear from heaven and will forgive their sins and restore their land. My eyes will be open and my ears attentive to every prayer made in this place. For I have chosen this Temple and set it apart to be holy—a place where my name will be honored forever. I will always watch over it, for it is dear to my heart. (**2 CHRONICLES 7:14-16**) **NLT**

**There is a way to heal the church
and to bring it back to some
semblance of its former glory.**

Dr. Gary Ray

GARY RAY
MINISTRIES

For God so loved the world
that He gave His only begotten Son,
that whoever believes in Him
should not perish but
have everlasting life.

- John 3:16

About The Author

Dr. Gary Ray is on a mission; a mission to spread the Truth and Good News of Jesus Christ to everyone! A great need exists today for truth to be spoken and he is up to the challenge. the Bible says in John 8:31(b)~32:

To the Jews who had believed him, Jesus said, "If you hold to my teaching, you are really my disciples. Then you will know the truth and the truth will set you free."

Ophelia & Gary Ray

Our modern-day society tends to "bend", shy away from, or "spin" the truth so it will be better received and more palatable. In many cases, the real truth gets diluted to the point where the original message is non-existent but in II Timothy 4:3~4 we read:

A time is coming when people will no longer listen to sound and wholesome teaching. They will follow their own desires and will look for teachers who will tell them whatever their itching ears want to hear. They will reject the truth and chase after myths.

Does this sound familiar?
Does this describe anyone you know?
Does this describe what is going on in your local church?

If so, they have rejected the truth and are chasing after myths.

At Gary Ray Ministries, we are committed to unapologetically teaching and preaching truth; truth that will set us free from the bondage of sin and death (John 8:34).

Truth sets us free, delivers us from our captive state and helps us realize the full potential freedom brings but non-truth keeps us in bondage and keeps us divided.

Dr. Gary Ray knows a little something about how truth can set a person free and release them into the fullness of what God has for their lives.

As a seasoned minister, Pastor, Teacher, Apostle, and Evangelist, Dr. Gary is taking his testimony "On the Road Again!" Through his testimony, he desires to see truth proclaimed and unity restored to the Body of Christ.

What Other's Say About Dr. Gary Ray

"Karen and I have known Dr. Gary Ray for several years. Dr. Ray's Life, testimony, and ministry are a God send to the body of Christ. Congratulations on your new book "Behind The Veil". I know this project was given to you by the Holy Spirit. Karen and I believe this book will stir the hearts of Pastors who read it. It's past time for the church of Jesus Christ to step up and step out. May God continue to bless you and your ministry."

Mark & Karen Poff
Pastors, New Harvest Ministries
Kingsport, TN.

"Dr. Gary Ray has been a spiritual father to many but especially for me over the last 25 years. I have always watched as he loved the church in many different capacities. For a while as a pastor, teacher, counselor, or friend. In his new book, Behind the Veil, Gary shows his concern for the church which I can say comes from his deep love of both the American church and God's people around the world. The truths he is revealing are necessary to hear to grow us into the ecclesia Jesus wanted us to be. This is the message we must preach, and Dr. Gary Ray does a brilliant job of laying the foundation for us. If we are to receive all God has for us, we must be found worthy to go Behind the Veil."

Tiffany Sweeley
Author, Singer, Minister & Counselor
Nashville, TN

"Behind the Veil is a timely writing for the current days we are living in. Its message is an important truth about the current "church" of these present times and its deceptions and snares. Many of today's ministries are wrapped up in conveniences and compromise ignoring the hidden dangers of" people pleasing "instead of God-pleasing.

"My long-time comrade in ministry and author, Dr. Gary Ray, is writing from the heart of God to warn, correct, and shed the light of God's word to the readers tying the Old Testament to the New Testament in the "tough "love and holiness God has intended from the beginning. He has a heart for the hurting and a burning desire to see the "church" become the "true" church once again. Behind the Veil is not only a must-read but a must-listen and obey read to come back to "Be Ye Holy as I Am Holy "says the Lord. Hebrews 13:8...Yesterday, today, forever Jesus is the same."

Marcia Ferko
Pastor, Greater Works Church
Columbus, OH

"Behind the Veal is an in-depth look at the position and condition of the church today. Jesus said to Peter "Upon this rock I will build my church". This book will take a hard look at the true meaning of building that church as Christ planned. Denominational doctrines, theological, and seminarial thinking were never a part of the foundational truths set forward by the Apostles of the first church.

"It is not that the author wants to change your mind or thinking of the church, but to give you, the reader more information to be able to make a more informed decision on what church should look like and whether the church you attend today has the same values as the first church. Today Dr. Ray shares the knowledge God has given him through so many years of service and experience to help bring the church back to its former glory."

Dr. Marshal V. Sherles
Maryville, TN

"Dr. Gary Ray has done it again, with another fabulous book about the state of the modern-day church – and it ain't pretty. Behind the Veil is a raw, "tell-it-like-it-and-don't-apologize" dissertation on how the church has lost its way. As the saying goes, "Truth is never popular", but Dr. Gary not only identifies the problem but also provides the solution. If you are struggling with what the church has become, this should be on your "must-read" list."

JK,
Cleveland, Ohio

"Dr Gary Ray, while serving as a chaplain for the Tennessee Rangers, has been a fantastic asset to us all. His newest book will bring his Scriptural guidance and insight to the church at large"

Major Chad Cantrell
1VTRS

"I believe the church has arrived at that pivotal point in history of final decision. Unfortunately, the choice has always been available and many within the body have made their decisions long ago.

Dr. Gary Ray's heart for the church and the decisions she has been making are very evident and compelling. He offers a simple solution."

Josh Singletary
Tribute Quartet, Inc.

Dr. Gary Ray and I (Bill Ray, Retired Banker Executive) have known each other for our entire lives. As kids, neighbors, playmates, veterans of many cowboy and Indian battles, and cousins, there has always been a close association though sometimes we were separated by geography. Our parents lived a few blocks apart, so we were constantly back and forth while playing during the early years. An early memory of Gary was of him gathering a few neighborhood kids under a tree and preaching to them.

At an early age he said that that is what he wanted to do in later life. This was probably the beginning of his awareness of God's call on his life. Over the years life took us in different directions. Gary joined the Navy which took him to Japan for a few years while I stayed in Tennessee and continued in school. Numerous jobs and family obligations, both good and bad, followed for both of us on different paths for many years but we would still be back in touch from time to time. The 15 years Gary spent in the gospel music business were a continuation of God's path for his life in a somewhat different form.

He was still traveling on God's path probably without realizing that some things were being put in place and others removed to fulfill the call which began under a tree on West Grundy Street in Tullahoma, TN. In Behind the Veil, Gary's view of the lack of involvement and dedication of churches in general calls for a total change in direction similar to the guidance in 2 Chronicles 7:14.

"If my people, which are called by my name, shall humble themselves, pray, and seek my face, and turn from their wicked ways, then I will hear from heaven, and will forgive their sin, and heal their land." 2 Chronicles 7:14

www.GaryRayMin.com

(615) 812-4279

www.ingramcontent.com/pod-product-compliance
Lightning Source LLC
Chambersburg PA
CBHW051250120626
46547CB00014B/1880